CW01513079

THIS ONE LIFE

Maria Iliffe-Wood

IW
Press

First Published in Great Britain by IW Press Ltd 2025

Cover graphic design: 1981D
Interior design: Chapter One Book Production

A catalogue record of this book is available from the British Library.

ISBN: 978-1-916701-11-3 (Paperback)
ISBN: 978-1-916701-12-0 (e-book)
ISBN: 978-1-916701-13-7 (Hardback)

IW Press Ltd
62-64 Market Street
Ashby de la Zouch
LE65 1AN

www.iliffe-wood.co.uk

For my dad
who continues to teach me from beyond the veil

PRAISE FOR *THIS ONE LIFE*

Since being asked to review this collection of poetry, it has rarely left my side. Over the past few weeks, it has been both a source of solace in moments of stress and a companion in quiet reflection. Iliffe-Wood offers a courageous and deeply personal exploration of vulnerability; delving into themes of identity, faith, and spiritual redemption.

Through poignant verses, she navigates her inner conflicts—battles with selfhood, ambition, and belief—ultimately guiding us toward a place of profound acceptance and grace. With striking honesty and insight, Iliffe-Wood reveals the transformative power of love and the quiet joy found in the present moment. This collection is not just a meditation on faith but a testament to the resilience of the human spirit.

—Professor Jonathan Vaughan, Principal,
Guildhall School of Music & Drama

This One Life is a bold look at bringing the divine into the daylight of our everyday lives. Maria twines her words around faith, feminism, and authentic self-religion, tightening her observations until they pop off the page. In *This One Life*, Maria has draped herself in vulnerability, writing her truth softly, doing the work of unravelling our questioning souls.

—Autumn Bettinger, Fishtrap Fellow, 2024.

Through this little book with a big soul, I got to know a different woman, a freer woman, a whole woman. The poems read as a search, a hunger to know in juxtaposition to a surrender of the sweetest kind. The woman I thought I was learning about was the author; the woman I got to know a little deeper was myself.

—JB Hollows, Mentor, Author of *Wing of an Angel*

In *This One Life*, Maria embarks on an odyssey that not only explores new form and expression in her writing, but is also a raw and visceral, deeply dense and personal examination of her being and very existence. Her work is dark, challenging, questioning, moving and soul searching. The elegies journey across 10 poems and the sense of a voyage is palpable throughout in language, form and feeling, and hits like a great tsunami crashing against the shore, before finally calming to a steady flow. Early on we are a given a hint of the raging torrent to come, "Frenzy hides behind a facade of gentle demeanour", and very quickly this façade is banished and we are exposed to the fire and force of feeling that rages below, like the earth's crust peeled back to reveal its fiery core. It is a brave and uncompromising examination of one's existence, questioning reality and even the presence of the Almighty. And although Death lingers inevitably as the final instalment, we can at least be heartened by the discoveries wrought from such an exacting endeavour, "The purpose of life, to love and be loved". These elegies deserve to be consumed as thoroughly as they have been written.

—Luke Shaw, Trainer, Therapist, Performer

The poems in *This One Life* spill from the author's generous spirit, landing as grace in the reader's heart and soul. Quiet yet resonant, reflective and searching, they weave a poetic tapestry stitched with threads of humble, deeply felt love.

—Linda Sandel Pettit, Ed.D., Author of *Leaning into Curves*, Speaker, and Spiritual Midwife

Powerful, inspiring deeply wrought and resonant words that remind us that poetry can be an act of re-remembering and re-connecting to all our parts on the journey of life.

—Cara Wheatley-McGrain Coach, Author, Speaker, Founder The Mindful Gut

It was a privilege to be asked to write a testimonial for Maria Iliffe-Wood's book, *This One Life*. Over the many years I've taught writing only four students have tackled Rilke's "Duino Elegies." Exploring the complexity of the ten poems is one thing but to study and write in the flavor of each is not a writing exercise for the faint of heart. In Iliffe-Wood's poems she demonstrates her awareness of what Rilke was aiming for. The deep philosophical excavating of themes flavored by death, angels, mortality, and love which represent the catalyst of Rilke's work. How Iliffe-Wood has been able to merge all these topics throughout the poems in *This One Life* is remarkable. At times the poems are filled with angst, the next moment hopefulness, followed by deep melancholy. This back and forth dance, like a human dances through the flawed emotional landscape of their own lives, reads on the page like a musical symphony. When I first received a copy of this book I walked around the house reading the poems out loud. It was a remarkable experience, at times feeling like the words were my own. I cannot recommend this series of poems enough.

—Jules Swales, Writing Teacher, Author of
Declarative and *I want a Stonehenge life*

Contents

Wholeness

I stare at the tree.
It teaches by its state of being.
Unaware of its given name.

Who would I be, if not Maria?
This name chosen for me.
This name I've worn like a velvet glove.

Maria. Not Marie.
Not even Ria.
No short form abbreviation,
know me only as my whole.

"Our Ria…" my dad said.
Dirty brown leather cowboy hat.
Calloused hands. Black oil under fingernails.
Smile as wide as a rainbow after the rain.
His love, as familiar
as the smell of noxious axle grease and tobacco
that emanated from his clothes.
"Yes," I said.

For whom but he could forestall the wrath of the iron
    maiden,
call me other than my given name
and yet know me for the whole of who I am.

Christened I was.
Seen by the father.
Held as and for God's child.
Mother Divine.
I declare myself whole.

Foreword

For many years, my writing voice has been pragmatic, down to earth. I write about ordinary, everyday matters and hope I show the extraordinary. I have been a student of writing for many years. Jules Swales, my teacher, suggested I study the *Duino Elegies*, by Rainer Maria Rilke, to help develop my writing. When I first read the *Elegies*, I couldn't fathom how I would ever write in such a dense, poetic way. The challenge was set, and I had to dig deep. I looked to my history and mined the depths of my soul.

I have asked questions for as long as I can remember. Why do I feel the way I feel? How do I get to feel better; more worthy? I wanted to understand why I had my life, and others had better lives. I pondered my human existence. I had questions about my spiritual nature, my purpose, the meaning of life. I switched between the idea of an omnipotent intelligence behind life, and the evidence of so much evil in the world that belied such an existence. I questioned myself: "Who I am?" … "Why am I here?"

Several years ago, I heard about Three Principles—introduced to the world by Sydney Banks—which provided some answers. With the understanding I gleaned from these principles, a ceasefire was called. A truce that my mind, in the main, has observed ever since. I took my hands off the steering wheel and life has taken some wonderful turns. Amazing things have transpired that came with as much ease as I've ever experienced.

These poems were inspired by the *Elegies*. As I wrote them, I pondered life's questions coupled with this spiritual understanding. As the poems emerged, I felt insights shift and reshape the insides of me—like my organs were being reshuffled to make life more comfortable.

I remain a work in progress. Even though I trust in the grace behind life, I sometimes feel I need to work at it; that success should not come easy, and, then, that prophesy becomes fulfilled.

Writing these poems, did not come easy—especially at the start. The ceasefire in my mind was broken for a short while, as I battled to understand what I was doing and felt the pressure to create something out of nothing.

The poems reminded me that was not my purpose. In fact, the poems reminded me of my insignificance. "I am not even a microscopic grain, a dot in God's eye." (*What the Dying Learn*) I felt liberation as I wrote that one sentence. As I let go of the illusion of control, I saw once again how the intelligence behind life has my back. Creative Genius put the words on the page, and as the battle in my head subsided, it became easier to pull the words out and put them together. After multiple iterations, I finally felt like the poems were complete.

I don't profess to know what life is about, yet I am grateful for the small amount of understanding that has been revealed—through the writing of these poems—from my soul. Now I present these poems to the world, in the hope that in the reading of them someone will see something helpful, something hopeful, something that has the power to transform a life.

Having said that, do not try to fathom an explanation from my words, rather let them wash over you, absorb them into your bones, let them seep into your being, and trust that

2

your mind will uncover perfect sense for you. I hope and pray that answers will come to questions you don't realise you're holding, and, in the reading, you feel a shift inside of you, a message from your soul, whereby you garner some meaning about life that may have eluded you thus far.

With love,

Maria Iliffe-Wood

Elusive Wisdom

Face values are nothing more
than dirty smears on a window,
grimy dissatisfaction to forestall the light.
Storm clouds of despair vent their fury
as the Ides of March.
Frenzy hides behind a facade of gentle demeanour.
Chagrined and fearful, heightened angst
does remonstrate against exacting arrows
that deflect existence.
Familiarity breeds;
algae on a stagnant pond.
Life's detritus leaves me festering,
incomplete, in need of suits of armour.
Caricatures designed to exaggerate
my worst or best.

Angels show themselves
to those with eyes to see.
God speaks in multiple languages.
The language of dreams,
flippant comments and psychics
or physics.

A wrecking ball flails through thoughts and dreams;
a catastrophe that belies
twenty-twenty vision.
Birds know the expansion of true nature.
Whoever told them they could fly
but I could not?

I drank the poisoned chalice.
Took to heart that which my soul knew
not to be true.
Threw God into the void.
While red Lucifer laughed.
Pain leaked from every pore.
Vision distorted by pungent castigation,
as I, wry with obdurate resolve,
stood firm in the atrocity of life.
Insight appears over the crucible,
veers towards the creative meanderings
of a nomadic heart.
Believes the resurrection and the light,
even as I turn my eyes away.

A lamb to the slaughter.
I walk towards the inevitable
in search of an answer,
to beseech release.

The invocation lands.
Ushered into the soundless void
to find the wisdom sought.
Yet wisdom is a face not recognised.
Veiled as it is by the mysterious night.
And I, afraid of the dark, weep as Mary
at the foot of the cross,
in the horror of the exalted dying.

A Feminine God

Caution is a byword.
Fear hidden dangers.
Protect yourself; menace lurks in the light.
Peter, the rock on which a church was built,
was a mere human who searched
for something beyond.

Hearts break for a sip of nectar
bestowed in moments of fragility.

Cracks in the glacier of a life
shamed into perfectionism.
Insights offer glimmers of hope.
Green shoots in the springtime.
Flowers after Enola Gay.
Divine faith is a chink of light behind a cloud.
Trust—a sprinkle of soft rain.
Riches we clamour to receive,
then cast aside like feed to the chickens.
Such realisations are larger than life, yet
this Ambrosia confers no immortality.

I yearn for weightlessness,
a lifetime of blessings contained in white silk.
This search has left me weakened.

I wish no more of it.
I surrender to a life carved out.

This meagre offering will have to suffice.
I can do no more.

Jesus, God's chosen son,
fell under the weight humanity
placed on his shoulders.
We, mere children of man,
were not born to bear this albatross.

A self, assembled with humble prayer,
inadequate, beseeches for that
which is most desired.
I wait in hope, faith and trust,
that answers will be furnished
before I take my final inhale.
God's blessing remains God's affair.

The Divine Feminine is kinder.
Mother God cradles our face in velvet palms,
renders tender smiles on human angst.
Her gentle eyes probe their way
through long assembled barriers
into my soul.
She looks upon the best and worst of me
and holds them one and the same.

This Mother God sits serene at my side,
trundles with me through the storm,
provides shelter through the furore
using her cloak of hope and faith,
a canopy of trust.

Hope, faith, and trust are not ours to own.
They are the blessing She bestows,
despite any rejections of such.
Hope, faith, and trust—
these Mother God wields on our behalf.
Only they hold the power to create universes;
a responsibility
I no longer bear as my own.

The Consequence of Innocent Decisions

A full-blooded female, with all the basic requirements
to fulfil the fervent desire of all women,
denied the ultimate creative act of this human form.
Readiness for the vastitude of life's creative forces
demanded a courage not forthcoming.
Many enter the field without fear.
Endure trials and tribulations,
foreseen and unforeseen
in the magnitude of what follows.
Destitution embroiled in responsibility for another's fate.

That churned and twisted internal view
became a guilt too heavy
to burden another innocent.
Shame! An unworthiness
I had no desire to bequeath.
Guilt and shame I locked
between my womb and my senses.
An existence expurgated
where mother and child became one and the same.

A decision, formed in unconsciousness,
a straitjacket for love, entangled as it was
in the anxieties and fears of a babe in arms.
Fate sealed in a child's eye impervious
to its repercussions.

Not God's will. No!
God's creativity
inexorable in the moment when formless
becomes form. What perfection that man
should be so designed
and woman too. Yet, this ball and chain
anchored in fake reality,
stripped licentious ecstasy.

O such decisions made in innocence.
Such dragons should be slain.
How cried the soul to expunge this wish.
Reached into the depths to extricate this misplaced
    aberration,
provided salve to the delicate bruises of the heart.
Returned to a new-born state,
to a time before the cross was laid bare,
where unbeknownst in that ere long moment,
the sweetness of gentle creation yet forever tainted.
Subdued yearnings a destiny.
Denouement a mix of guilty pleasure and shame.

Jealous for she who languished
in her womanhood without moderation.
Pleasure, a secret oblivion,
incarcerated in silken folds.
Sounds of the flesh ruptured in her throat,
then retreated to whence they came.

Angel feathers glide and softly touched
on Mother Nature's soil.
Let go the crusade.

Divine pleasure freed to swim, to soar,
to float in the warm waters of the abyss.
Light led to a place where fruitful expression
enjoys the purity of unconditional joy.
And yet, prior destiny. This sweet maiden,
so drilled in fear of consequence,
denied motherhood
and in so doing denied herself.

What The Dying Learn

God created darkness.
Souls half-hidden by shade.
Fear laced it with punitive dragons.
Life breathes in its shadows,
half breaths. Unworthy a desultory taste.
NOT ENOUGH sculpted across a heart,
carved by the chisel of maternal instincts.

The weight of being a good mother,
a hammer on chisel, used indiscriminately
in the hope of doing the right thing.
No mother can deliver on that promise,
in the eyes of her child.

Her tools carved this burdensome adult
from the clay of innocence.
Her words, fissures in the marble,
shadows from the tree
of misguided protection,
cracks plastered over with Band-Aid.
A life of jagged edges.

Life drew blood and deemed me unworthy.
We're all damaged goods. Am I right?

There is not a one amongst us wholly perfect.
We are all flawed.

Jesus died on the cross for our sins,
yet man hoisted the petard
for the misdemeanours of Adam and Eve.
Damned me to a factitious Gehenna.
A shadowland
with no light to guide me home.

I built this purgatory with my own hands,
bloodied and torn from the effort.
I bear the scars with fortitude, with pride.
The effort exhausts me, yet I persevere.
I laid brick upon brick to build walls,
that later I dismantled.

Offload this hammer and chisel,
passed down through the blood of ancestors.
Stop carving out a bad deal.
O to shed new light on this tiny span of existence.
This oh so short life.
This microscopic grain,
not even a dot in God's eye.
Compare pi to eternity and
we don't even come close.

Is this what the dying learn?

The Fight for Control

A threat hangs like a cadaver on the gallows,
a stark harbinger of what may come.
Goliath's David, my Delilah,
to strip away all I travail for.
My reward in this life compensated
with damnation in the next.
The afterlife a noose awaiting
the nod from the hangman's master.

Still waters await the drop of a pebble,
that wreaks a tsunami of havoc.
The eye of the storm is a thief in the night.
A mirage of tranquillity forebodes the cyclone ahead.
One-hundred-foot waves smash this skiff to smithereens.
The life I dreamed of
shattered in the blink of an eye.

The yoke borne across these shoulders,
drags chains of discontent and vicissitudes,
a mutation of what may be.
Life is not to be trusted.
I must be in control.

Try hard. Work hard.
Dictums etched across my forehead,

laced with the promise of rewards, undefined.
The challenge accepted,
long before the meaning was made clear.
A constant grasping
for jewels beyond my reach,
a word on the tip of my tongue
that refuses to reveal itself.
Desires fulfilled only for the deserving.
History dictates,
those who work hardest reap the largest bounty.
Therein a sentence to a lifetime of hard labour.

Such heinous felony rendered this innocent
to incur so severe a penalty.
A guileless crime committed in the cradle
before conventions elucidated,
corroborated and entrenched
through the verbiage of ages.

Tell me though.
Could I yet shape a cloud in the heavens?
Or chisel a wave from the ocean?
These, no more attainable than
carving out my destiny.
I cannot be sure fate will deliver
that for which I pray,
yet prayer be my only recourse.

Fear—my annihilation.
I trust the intelligence of life to let me down,
no leading to green pastures,
led instead, at breakneck speed,
to false promises and grim times.
Led to a life not of abundance,
but of poverty and drear.

I fear my destiny is destitution.
A monstrous failure—a life in ruins.
This be a prerequisite for my evolution?
No. I cannot, will not, take the chance.
I will not allow life's hands on the steering wheel.
I will exert my control.
Even with the notion;
it is a veiled and perpetuated fallacy.

What is Reality?

A compelling force leads to spurious truth,
like a hangman's noose, choking.
Dragging me into an oblivion I welcome
willingly and in innocence.
Conditioned to believe the best is found
in a moonless night.

I fumble around,
strive for the light I left behind.
Hackles rise, composure unbalanced.
A yoke placed on my shoulder,
a force pushes and shoves,
discombobulates, and tells me:

THIS.

THIS IS REAL.

THIS IS REALITY.

I acquiesce. Follow the instruction to strive.
Fight. Bludgeon ahead.
"Where's forward?" I scream into the void.
Arms flail, clutch for tenure.
An abyss looms below my feet.
Manacled. No compass bearing.

Propelled into delusion.
A phantasm of distance travelled.

I wail for guidance.
Pray for my blighted existence.
Blindness shuts me down
in shame and guilt.
Delilah has cut me off at the roots.
I cower—at her feet.

Foetal.
I sink inside myself.
Hide my shame.
Close my eyes to the outside world.
Fold arms around my body.
Curl into a ball.
Pray for the sleep of the dead.

And as I pray,
and as I close my eyes and see inside,
and as I fall asleep,
a calmness forms a warm bath around my soul,
a suffusion of white silk.
Smooth caramel floats through my veins.
Contentment a star gazer lily with pink at the edges,
full of ripe pollen.

Cradled in eternity's womb.
A bubble of serenity.
The past recedes.
The future disappears.

All there is, is now.
All I am is now.
I am.   Now.

Is There a Higher Power?

Ye who whispers in silence,
hides inside metaphor,
in leaves that blow in the wind,
in the soft touch of a butterfly wing
on the hairs of my arm,
hides the secret where no human will glance.

The search blinkered by
insecurity and indecision
about who I am.
Sixty years and the struggle
for answers persists.
Answers that demand much of this humble flesh.

Wretched. I stand in awe
of the magnificence behind life,
yet demand proof of its existence.
Question all atrocities,
man pitched against man,
yet take comfort that,
with hindsight, reason will prevail.
Assert that all is as it should be,
despite apocalypse, ruin and warfare,
yet appeal for an end to barbarity.

Belief is a choice that does not require truth.
Blessed are those who do not believe,
for they shall walk in ignorance their entire life.

Let not suffering be the conduit
to all that needs to be discerned.
Hands clutch for explanations
not forthcoming, grasp, with desperation,
their existence, quarry to heinous opinions
unbecoming of a faithful soul
that longs to be known, longs to be cherished,
longs to bask in the grace of angels.
Hearts ache in the need for eternal peace,
yet tremble under God's kiss.

Accord me a glimpse of those rooms
in the father's mansion, outside of consciousness,
a chink in the wall,
a crack through which I glimpse the eternal,
where she is seated,
still and patient.
Her for whom time is of no essence.
She who will wait through eternity,
and it will be soon enough.

Traverse me the interminable journey
from head to heart,
the place where abundance, grace and ease
abide in harmony.

Give not commandments set in stone,
lead instead to comprehension
of fervent assiduity.

Be not vague of mind.
Land me safe and sound in certitude.

Bring me knowing,
without ignorance.

Show me your face,
not in icons,
rather let me look into your eyes
and see infinity.

Search for a Life of Ease

Blessed are God's creatures
who rest in the simplicity of their essence,
the fecundity of their existence.
No question of incurring the wrath of God.
Ire does not exist.
Sin does not exist.
A life unburdened by manmade complexity.

Man did choose this clouded life.
Put ourselves above God's creatures,
crowned ourselves with a lifetime of labour.
Took ourselves out of the now
into a life yoked with tar and feathers,
a hung, drawn and quartered existence.

Our forefathers chose this life,
riddled with the past,
forfeited for the future,
dismissive of the now.
In so doing, set the precedent
for all generations to follow.

'What is'—subsumed
by the nature of our personal mind.

Attention fettered by expectations
of gargantuan proportions.
Forget what is.
Strive for endless possibility
or entitlement. Stand oblivious
in a self-made mire,
while hearts yearn for the glaring obvious.

O for that lack of chicanery, lack of guilt,
a life without extrapolation.
No junctures. No mediocrity to overcome.
No angst.
No angst.
No angst.
No mantras. No affirmations.
No convincing myself that all is well.

For God's blessed creatures,
death has no prominence,
no fearful glance.
When death is nigh,
there are no regrets.

O to look death full in the face,
cite John Keats and have
no fear that I may cease to be.

Aforetime, we knew this experience of what is.
Born into the silence of what is.
With dying breaths do we not go back
to that place of what is.
Angst leaves of its own free will.
Deadlines. Milestones. Goals.
All jurisdictions beyond feeble intelligence.
In feeble lies unutterable strength.
In feeble intelligence lies freedom.

A febrile mind burdened as it is,
does not have the ability
to notice the now.

Open up to the now.
Rise when the sun rises,
sleep when the sun sleeps,
eat when hungry,
sing, sing, sing to heart's content.

Open your eyes,
pull back the curtains of your soul,
allow the light of what is to seep in.

Open to the magnificence of nature,
the munificence of what is,
the beneficence with which you are blessed.

Regain the eternal blessedness
granted to all God's creatures,
of which I am one.

This One Life

Children laugh and play
in a rusted tin bath
by the side of a Ugandan road.
Surrounded by tumbledown shacks
and abject poverty.

Watch as a mother sponges the red dust
from her child's soft brown skin.
She lilts an African melody,
sprinkled with clicks and whispers.

The child's eyes dance.
The mother's eyes dance,
in a way that my eyes haven't danced
in the longest time.
No poverty of spirit here.
Abundance lies in the eyes of that child, that mother.
What is this life, if not to laugh?

And yet.
Are we to enjoy only the salutary moment?
Is that what living is?
Or experience whatever is, in the moment;
anger, frustration, jealousy,
fear, judgement.

These too, part of a life lived.
Not one amongst us
will lie on our deathbed
having experienced only joy.

Do not value only good moments
and discard the rest.
And in so doing, lay to waste
much of this transient life.

I will not do that.

Will not judge myself, nor others,
for my judgement.
Will not be angry at myself, or others,
for my anger.
Will not be saddened by moments of grief.
Will not wish for an alternate emotion.

This I understand.
Without grief, I know not joy.
Without anger, I do not recognise calm.
Without judgement I will not discern opposites.
Without choice I have no free will to decide
how to live these God-given moments
of this one life.

Do not lose this one life
to fear of death. Lose life
to the desire to achieve. Lose life
to the human capacity to strive and grieve.
Do not lose this one life,
to graft and turmoil,
yearning for something
other than what is.

In a life lived in acceptance
of what is
does joy appear.
In the knowledge of our final hour
does calm contentment arise.
A feeling of love, peace and gratitude,
our guide throughout this one life.

This life that once stretched
a million years into infinity,
now cascades like water through my fingers.
A tiny drop left
in the palm of my hand,
which cannot be held forever.

Watch the flower bloom.
Watch the birds build their nest.
Watch the tree reside in magnificence.

Watch the child play,
the mother sing.
Observe the serenity,
here within us.

Observe the silence,
the backdrop.
And in the silence.
Be.

This.
One.
Life.

Death

Death, the most egregious affair, loiters.
When Death arrives,
what do we carry with us?
Grief. Angst. Anger toward our fellow man.
The judgement laid at our door.
The lack.

What part grief in the evolution of our soul?
What part anger, jealousy, frustration, depression?
All in equal measure part of this existence.
Yet treated with contempt.
A dirty word, shunned by satirical judgement.
A private affair,
to be experienced behind closed doors.
Do not step this demonic possession
into the public domain.
Beseech not the understanding
of fellow human beings.

Yet, I implore.
Bear with the reality of these demons.
Do not fear the apocalypse.
Think you not crazy
when these doorways are revealed,
for doorways they are.

Transmutation is not an easy ride.
Invite it to the table.
Be open to its intention.
Hear beyond its fatalistic verbiage.

Seek not only pleasant moments.
Rely not only on joy and happiness.
Regret not those despised thoughts or
emotions you sought to expel,
as you played judge, jury, and executioner.
Damn not your soul to eternal angst.
Guilt and shame
are handcuffs to this one existence.

Face the behemoth and seek its value,
without layers of distorted meaning.
Have no fear in this endeavour.
I will hold you in my embrace,
gift you with love,
while you make this transition.

Heal scars through love.
Heal grief through love.
Heal sadness through love.
Heal anger through love.
Jealousy, frustration, depression,
anxiety, fear, loathing,
guilt, shame, hostility.
All shall be experienced and
healed through love.

Love measured only
by the depths to which one has fallen
and given without condition,
without judgement, without blame.
We harm ourselves enough

with these three swords of Damocles.

The purpose of life,
to love and be loved.

Let not one scar appear
on another's soul,
smote by your malice.
Let not one heart
be encumbered by contempt.
Let not one life be oppressed by greed.
Let not your one life be a blight on another's.

Show kindness
where there is pain and hurt.
Compassion
where there is grief and sadness.
Be peace in the midst of war.
Generosity in poverty.
Be a shining light of joy and contentment
in a world bereft.
Love where there is hate.

Live from love.
Not tough love,
not killing with kindness.

Be sweetness of heart,
kindness of tongue,
gentleness of touch
that is love and only love.

When Death arrives
let the one thing you carry
from this life to the next

be love.

A Word for Writers

I am a student of Jack Grapes Method Writing, as taught by Jules Swales. For two seasons I studied the *Duino Elegies* by Rainer Maria Rilke. This study forced me to dig deep into my psyche to excavate fundamental questions about human existence. I started with no idea about what to write.

Existential questions appeared on the page, posed so that creative genius might show up with an answer. Yet the answers were not obvious and did not come from my intellect.

This writing stretched and challenged my writing capabilities. The process was different from any writing process I had followed before. My process has been different for each of the books I have written and published. This was by far the most strenuous!

The poems are the result of mammoth revisions and editing. None of the pieces came out whole. They are fragments of many thousands of words that appeared on the pages. Many hours were spent pulling out small sentences, selected paragraphs, words from here and there, chopping, shaving, carving, crafting, moving and re-moving until eventually the poem showed me what it wanted to be. I imagine this akin to the work of Michelangelo when he found the David in the marble. Whilst I do not profess to be a Michelangelo, I will say that I am immensely proud of these poems.

Maria Iliffe-Wood

Connect with Maria

Did you enjoy *This One Life*?
Reviews make all the difference as to how well a book makes its way out into the world. If you enjoyed this book, and especially if it made an impact on you, I would be a very happy author if you could leave an honest review on your reading platform of choice.

If you'd like to know more about me and what I'm doing in the world, you can connect with me in a variety of places:

Follow me on Facebook: www.facebook.com/iliffewood

To read more of my creative writing, subscribe on Medium: https://medium.com/@maria_32943

To find out what else I do in the world, check out my website: www.iliffe-wood.co.uk

Sign up to Book Matters newsletter for writing and publishing hints and tips: https://iliffe-wood.co.uk/newsletter

If you're working on a book project, the Write Community might be just the support and encouragement you need: https://www.iliffe-wood.co.uk/the-write-community

What to Read Next

Books by Maria Iliffe-Wood

A Caged Mind: How Spiritual Understanding Changed a Life
Daily Yarns: Riding the Lockdown Rollercoaster of Emotions
Coaching Presence: Building Consciousness and Awareness
    into Coaching Interventions

Anthologies published by the IW Press / Jules Swales Partnership

Lies, Lies and More Lies: How to Create and Build Fictional
    Characters
Stories from the Muses: Become a Better Writer
A Different Story: How Six Authors became Better Writers

Books published in partnership with IW Press Ltd

Cosmic Collect Call: Appreciate the Mystery, Poems about Life
    by Renuka O'Connell
Declarative: 33 Statements that Changed My Life by Jules
    Swales
Leaning into Curves: Trusting the Wild Intuitive Way of Love by
    Linda Sandel Pettit
Wing of an Angel: An Exploration of Human Potential in the
    Back of Beyond by JB Hollows
The Should Stick: Stop Being a People Pleaser by Tracey
    Hartshorn

About Maria Iliffe-Wood

I LOVE writing. I love books. I love helping other people to write and publish their books. I love talking about writing. When I talk about writing, I feel myself light up in a way I don't light up for any other part of my life.

I didn't set out to be a writer, or an author, or even a publishing partner, but when I look back at the breadcrumb trail, I see that it was always on the cards.

The person I most associated with in my young life was Anne Frank. I thought it was because she had a difficult relationship with her mother, and because she felt trapped in ways that I felt trapped in my life. When I look back now, I realise it was because she felt a need to write. To get down on paper her innermost thoughts and feelings. I suspect she learned a lot about herself as she wrote. Or maybe I'm just projecting that onto her, because that's what happens for me.

I was 52 years old when I published my first book. For that book I took a deep reflective dive into my coaching practice and, boy, did I learn a lot about coaching and presence in writing that book. At the time I believed it was the only book I would ever write.

Life sure did have some surprises in store for me. Now I'm the sole author of four books, and a contributing author to another three. Whilst each book is different, every one of them has entailed some kind of deep dive into aspects of my life. In the writing I have learned so much about myself and how life works. This is why I keep writing.

I've also published three anthology books which include stories from twenty-six authors, most of whom were first-time authors. I see these anthologies as a stepping stone to the writers having the confidence to publish their own work. I'm delighted that some of them have already done that, and some of them are on their way. I've partner published several books for authors. Books that are having a significant impact on the world.

I live in Leicestershire, England. If you stick a pin in the middle of a map of England, you will find me right there! I live with my husband, Ashley Wood, without whom none of my writing would exist in the world.

Appreciation

First my dear friend Jules Swales, who also happens to be my writing teacher. Without you none of my creative writing would exist in the world. When we made that first connection over breakfast in Seattle in 2018, neither of us had any idea where this friendship would take us. Thank you for your teaching, your support, your encouragement, your sage advice, and, most of all, for being the person that you are. What a journey we have had together, and long may it continue.

Jacqueline Hollows, (JB Hollows), my gosh, what a friendship we have. I am so grateful for your wisdom, your cheerleading, your endless optimism, and your loving friendship. I learn so much from you in every conversation we have. The way you approach life and work is an inspiration to me. I am grateful that even a fraction of it has rubbed off on me. I love how, when we work together, how easy we rub along. Working with you doesn't feel like work.

Linda Sandel Pettit, Ed.D. You are many things in the world, including an inspirational leader, creative guide, and, not least, in my eyes anyway, my friend. I am so grateful for your loving and constructive creative developmental feedback for *This One Life*. You have a knack of seeing and highlighting the best of my writing, and also showing me where it can be better. I love you as my editor and as a presence in my life.

Michael Pastore. Proofreader extraordinaire, and all round nice person. Your attention to detail is extraordinary. Thank you for picking up the holes in this manuscript. It wouldn't be the same without you.

Catherine Williams. I am so pleased I found you for the design of the interior of my books. You do such a great job, as well as being a delight to work with. I so appreciate your patient responses to my to-ing and fro-ing with changes of mind, and your guidance when my ideas won't work!

Iain Hill. Another gem. Thank you for finding me! I don't usually respond to direct marketing, but when yours dropped in my letterbox, something about it connected. It's great to work with you. You do a fabulous job of the cover designs. Thank You.

Vickie Boff. A year ago, I knew nothing about Amazon Advertising. I thought it would be an easy way to sell books! Little did I know. Thank you so much for your guidance helping me get to a stage where they might even be working. You've been a pleasure to talk to and to learn from.

The Write Community. My small, but perfectly formed band of writers. Meeting with you twice-monthly keeps me on my toes and motivated to show up for my writing as much as for yours.

Jack Grapes, whom I have never met, spoken to, or had any kind of interaction with, yet I am grateful for him and his creation of Jack Grapes Method Writing, which has transformed my writing and brought me to where I am now.

Mandy and Lorraine, Jenny and Ken, you might not have contributed to the book directly, but you are my support network, and without that, the book would not be in existence. I'm sorry I spend so much time twittering on about all things writing. Lucky for me, if I'm boring you to tears, you do a good job of hiding it!

My family. The Iliffes, the Woods and all their respective partners. There are too many of you to name, and you know who you are. I love you all.

Ashley Wood. I love you most of all. Thank you for EVERYTHING.

* * *